The Teen Witches'

Manifesting

Written by Claire Philip
Illustrated by Luna Valentine

ARCTURUS

SAFETY WARNING

This book features activities that involve the use of candles, paper, lighters, matches, herbs, oils, resins, and other similar materials. Always consult an adult before working with any of these items. Never light candles on or near anything that can catch fire. Never leave a candle burning unattended. Keep candles away from small children and animals.

The ideas, suggestions, and activities in this book are not intended to be a substitute for conventional medical advice. Always consult your doctor or other qualified healthcare professional before undertaking any alternative therapy to ensure that there are no contraindications for your health.

ARCTURUS

This edition published in 2023 by Arcturus Publishing Limited
26/27 Bickels Yard, 151–153 Bermondsey Street,
London SE1 3HA

Title Adapted from *The Essential Book of Mindfulness* by Wendy Hobson, *Ultimate Book of Spells* by Pamela Ball, and *Spells for Mindfulness* by Pamela Ball.

Author: Claire Philip
Illustrator: Luna Valentine
Designer: Rosie Bellwood
Editors: Donna Gregory and Rebecca Razo
Editorial Manager: Joe Harris
Indexer: Lisa Footitt

ISBN: 978-1-3988-2567-3
CH010879NT
Supplier 29, Date 0123, PI 00002503

Printed in China

Contents

This icon indicates the use of candles, lighters, and matches. Have an adult supervise you when working with these materials, and use caution.

What is Manifesting?

Introducing Manifestation

"Manifestation" and "manifesting" are real buzz words these days! This is because people are discovering that they have the power to change their lives.

This book discusses how to train the brain to become mindful, so that you can quiet your thoughts and take deliberate steps toward creating the life you really want.

Mindfulness is an important part of manifesting, as it can help you connect with the world around you. From a peaceful yet alert state, you can spot opportunities when they show up and make the best decisions for you.

FINDING POSITIVITY

Mindfulness also brings a boost of positive energy!
Optimism is an important part of manifestation—
you must believe that something better is possible.

Over time, and through concentration, you can
learn to become fully present. You can find where
you are holding tension and then release it, so that
you can move more calmly and confidently
through life.

We can only manifest
our true desires from a
place of peace, and that's
why mindfulness and
meditation are key.

What is Mindfulness?

Introducing Mindfulness

Mindfulness is concentrating all your awareness on whatever you are doing at any one moment.

You can be mindful while sipping a hot drink, watching the birds from your window, or while cleaning, working, cooking, or even reading this book! The important thing is

that all your attention is directed at whatever you are doing in the moment—without thinking about the other things you could, or should, be doing. It is allowing all of the thoughts that naturally arise in your mind to pass through—without following them.

"What is this life if full of care,
we have no time to stand and stare?"
—William Henry Davis

BEING PRESENT

Part of becoming more mindful is not dwelling on the past or looking too far into the future. When we look backward too often, we tend to turn over events in our minds and wish things could have been different. If we think about the future too much, we can easily project our worries—and then suffer in the present.

By embracing mindfulness, we can experience more of the world's beauty. Mindfulness takes us away from judgment and fear so that we can see things as they are. This is key for manifestation—it helps us achieve a more content mind. What's not to love about that?

Research has shown
that mindfulness is effective for

- Helping with pain
- Coping with mental-health issues
- Easing the effects of long-term illnesses
- Improving well-being

Elements of Mindfulness

Being nonjudgmental is one of the most important parts of mindfulness. This is because to be truly mindful, we need our thoughts and our feelings to be balanced.

Mindfulness can also help us:

- Meditate to find inner calm
- Acknowledge and respect our emotions—and understand how individual emotions make us feel
- Release emotions so they do not control us
  - Value stillness and quiet
  - Respond thoughtfully to situations
  - Leave uncomfortable memories behind
  - Release the need to think constantly about the future
  - Let go of our blocks

MEDITATION

Most people begin their mindfulness journey by learning to meditate. Meditating is a way of quieting your thoughts so that you can experience a deep feeling of calm. This can take a little time, and everyone's meditation experience is different. Take it at your own pace. See page 30 for a simple technique to get you started.

After meditating for a while, you'll start to notice your experiences with less emotion. For example, before meditating you may feel angry at a friend for a blunt text, but after meditating you may see that they were stressed out, tired, or in a rush.

Looking at situations as they are—without judgment—helps you stay cool, calm, and collected. This is the first step to manifesting the things you want.

The Origins of Mindfulness

While we don't know the exact origin of mindfulness, we do know that it has been around since ancient times. Ancient Greek philosophers believed every person should seek happiness by making the most of every moment.

Greek philosopher Epictetus understood that the way we perceive the world around us greatly affects our understanding of reality: "What concerns us is not the way things actually are, but rather the way we think things are."

The surviving writings of one Roman emperor, Marcus Aurelius, show that he believed people should develop a positive attitude and not allow negative thoughts to take hold and control their personality.

BUDDHISM AND MINDFULNESS

Mindfulness is at the heart of Buddhist philosophy and is one of the eight principles that the Buddha taught people to follow.

These eight principles are:

- Understanding
- Intention
- Speech
- Action
- Livelihood
- Effort
- Mindfulness
- Concentration

Following a Buddhist path means putting these skills into play with the intention of achieving the ultimate aim—finding happiness. Mindfulness is a key part of this. Buddhists use meditation to change their thought processes—which then changes their perception of the world.

> The Buddha believed that we can change our circumstances by changing our thoughts and our attitude.

SO WHY DO WE NEED MINDFULNESS?

Because most of us are experiencing far too much stress! One of the reasons for this is the advancement of modern technology. We always have access to an overwhelming amount of information—and this can throw us off.

While technology has given us so much, it has also created problems that we haven't come across before. Technology has influenced every area of our lives, and now most people rely on their smart phones for maps, paying for things, texting, listening to music—and so much more. We can access all these things, including the Internet, in seconds—this has made us impatient for instant solutions.

Have you ever felt any of the following pressures?

- to have the latest phone, clothes, or shoes

- to achieve your goals quickly

- to do everything fast

- to always be productive

- to take part in the latest exercise or diet trend

Trying to keep up with our fast-paced world can lead to over-thinking, confusion, and inaction— none of which gets you anywhere. It is also very time-consuming!

Social Media

While social media has many advantages, such as keeping in touch with people all over the planet, it also presents us with an unrealistic view of the world. What people post online is highly selective—they choose what to share about themselves.

Think about it—people are far more likely to post a photo of a happy moment with friends than an image of them stressed out about exams at 10 pm.

Mindfulness doesn't mean unplugging from social media—but it does ask us to be watchful of how we use it, what we are feeling when we use it, and how we react to those feelings.

The next time you go on social media, try to bring yourself into a state of awareness by noticing:

- Why you are scrolling
- If you are doing something purposeful (for example, looking up a recipe)
- What you are feeling
- Whether your mood is affected
- The amount of time you spend on social media
- How you feel afterward

Part of mindfulness is working out whether you feel better or worse from an experience. Monitor how you feel on social media, and begin to make more deliberate choices around who you follow—and why.

Feeling Stressed

Stress isn't always a big problem—it is a part of life, and we can cope with a certain amount. Stress only becomes an issue when pressure becomes overwhelming. The side effects of stress can be physical or mental, and they will be different for everyone. Here are ways stress can affect us:

Living In The Past

When trying to cope with modern life, it is natural for people to turn to their old ways of doing things; however, this can mean always getting the same unhelpful results.

Feeling Down

Having more than your fair share of down days or serious mental-health problems can come from too much stress. Sometimes, a particular event (or series of events) can trigger a problem or severely affect your confidence.

Difficulty Sleeping

If you are feeling tense, you may find it difficult to sleep or to get a good night's sleep.

Mindfulness is available to people of all backgrounds. By cultivating awareness in the present moment, we gain understanding, confidence, and a positive outlook.

What Happens When We Meditate?

Thanks to scientific studies, we know that during meditation our brains move between concentration and distraction.

The more we do our meditation the less distracted we become. This is because meditation can change the way the brain works. Meditation influences our brain-wave patterns and encourages concentration, emotional control, and thoughtful decision-making. For this to happen, mediation needs to be regular and ongoing.

Brain waves are electrical pulses that pass between parts of the brain. The frequency of the pulse determines the type of brain wave.

- BETA WAVES pulse at 14–30Hz when we are awake, alert, and attentive.
- ALPHA WAVES pulse at 8–14Hz when we are relaxed but alert.
- THETA WAVES pulse at 4–8Hz when we are drowsy.
- DELTA WAVES pulse at 0.5–4Hz when we are in deep sleep.

RESEARCH RESULTS

A Norwegian study compared the brain waves of experienced meditators when they were meditating compared to when they were resting.

This is what they found:

- The lack of delta waves during meditation and rest proved that sleep has a different effect on the brain than resting or meditation.
- Alpha waves associated with relaxed attention were strongest when subjects were meditating.
- Theta waves were strongest during rest.

The study showed that sleep, rest, and meditation have three definite effects on the brain.

People suffering from depression or anxiety tend to have more activity on the right side of the brain, rather than the left (which is the norm). Further studies have shown that people who meditate have more activity on the right side, which suggests that it could help enhance mood and lift depression.

Mindfulness
in Action

Changing Attitudes

We can't change everything in life so that our outcomes are always good—many things are outside our control. The sooner we learn to approach these challenges with a better mindset, the easier life can be.

For example, you discover that you have to work on a project with someone you find annoying. You can't change the other person's personality, so you can make a choice: either continue to feel negative or try a mindful approach. Instead of stewing in your unpleasant feelings, gossiping, or being unkind, you can meditate on the emotions you feel, acknowledge them fully, and then put them aside.

"You can't stop the waves, but you can learn to surf."
— Jon Kabat-Zinn

MINDFUL ACTIVITY

If you are bothered by someone, go into meditation, and
ask yourself when you first felt that way. Maybe someone
else in the past has acted similarly and you are seeing
a pattern–or maybe they are showing a characteristic
that you have inside you that you don't particularly like.
Reflecting in this way gives you power over the situation
and can help you move forward in a constructive way.

Managing Pain

As well as pain caused by sprains, bruises, cuts, and breaks,
physical pain can also be caused by tension and stress. The
mindful approach to this kind of pain is to calm the brain
waves through meditation.

Mindfulness helps ease pain—such as tension
headaches—caused by too much stress
by encouraging us to concentrate on
the moment, rather than the pain.
This enhances brain-wave patterns
that strengthen
positive
thoughts
and
distract
from the
pain itself.

Always
seek
professional
help for any kind of
physical or mental-
health issue.

Meditation can also help some
long-term illnesses by reducing
tension held in the body. General mood plays a huge part in
many conditions, and if people can maintain a meditation
habit that slows their brain waves and brings a sense of calm,
discomfort and pain can slowly begin to ease.

MENTAL HEALTH

Mental health is just as important as physical health. It's very important that anyone who experiences anxiety or depression is taken seriously. Luckily, there are many therapies that have had great success in helping people feel better.

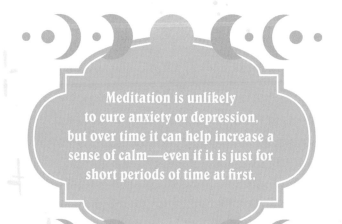

Meditation is unlikely to cure anxiety or depression, but over time it can help increase a sense of calm—even if it is just for short periods of time at first.

MINDFUL ACTIVITY

Journaling is a great way to process and release emotion. Simply take a notebook and write a few pages of whatever comes to mind, ideally in the morning. You can rip up the pages afterward if you want to–the key is to write whatever is swirling around in your mind and taking up your mental energy.

A MEDITATION FOR UNCOMFORTABLE FEELINGS

Leo Babauta is an author who writes on mindfulness. Here is his method if you are feeling stressed, frustrated, lonely, sad, or tired.

- Notice that you're feeling a difficult emotion and acknowledge how it feels in your body.
- Notice any thoughts behind the emotion, and write them down. For example, you might be feeling sad but thinking, "They shouldn't be treating me this way."
- Notice that your thoughts are causing the difficulty more than the situation itself. This might be hard to see at first.
- Ask yourself, "What would it be like if I didn't have these thoughts right now?" This helps you see that you are separate to your emotions.
- Begin to see that this experience is neither good nor bad—it just is—and that you are feeling a strong emotion.

This technique is worth the time spent for the awareness it brings. While you might not be able to completely let go of an emotion, you will begin to learn that the kind of thoughts you attach to a situation greatly impact how you experience it.

Anger Management

Anger that gets out of control is rarely a solution to a problem—and usually only makes things worse! If you can learn to step back from a situation that has made you lose your temper, and then release your emotions, you should be able to handle stressful situations more easily.

Anger is a very strong emotion, so it's best to take things slowly. When you are meditating, think about what has upset you, and try to distance yourself from it by imagining that you are watching it on a movie screen or television. If you feel your anger rising, breathe deeply and slowly five times—then try again. Now imagine yourself coping in a calm, rational way to whatever you are facing.

Some people find anger very difficult because as children they were taught it was a "bad" emotion. This isn't the case—anger is an important emotion that tells us something is not as it should be.

MINDFUL ACTIVITY
If you feel too angry to quiet your mind, you can also journal, dance to loud music, stomp your feet, create a dramatic piece of art, shout into a pillow, or even punch a cushion. The important thing here is to express your anger in a safe way. Some people even smash up melons!

CONTROLLING FEAR
Fear is another extremely intense emotion that is difficult to experience. Meditation can help you realize that fear often begins—and is built up—in the mind. As you observe your thoughts, you'll notice how they sometimes build up your fears. In time, you can let them pass by without taking you over.

Enjoying the Moment

To be mindful, we must learn to observe and enjoy what is in front of us right now. So often we are thinking about something else and become distracted by thoughts of the past or future.

> Mindfulness can help us look at everything without judgment. If there is something we cannot change, the only thing we can do is alter the way we look at it.

If we turn an issue or incident over and over in our mind, it will only make us more anxious. Increased anxiety leads to even more concern and worry—and we don't want that!

Instead, we can look at whatever is causing us stress and acknowledge our part in it—what we did and how it made us feel. Having acknowledged what happened, we can think new thoughts that don't feed the cycle of worry.

CREATIVITY

How does this all relate to manifestation? Being able to enjoy the moment often means that you can access creativity. This is because you are feeling more relaxed and able to look outward. When we are calm and present, we can take better care of ourselves, come up with ideas, plan, and act—all of which is extremely hard if we are suffering.

Assess Your Personality

Try answering the following questions in a journal:

- How would you describe yourself in a few words?
- What are your strengths?
- Is there anything you struggle with?
- How are your relationships with friends and family?
- Do you make new friends easily?
- What do others expect of you?
- What do you expect of others?
- Are you cautious when meeting new people?
- Do you have a strong self-image?
- Do you find it hard to concentrate?
- Do you enjoy silence?

Compare your answers in three months' time to see if things have changed after you've developed a meditation habit.

Moving Through Blocks to Meditation

In an ideal world, you would meditate for 10–30 minutes each day; however, this can be difficult if your routine is varied. Start with 10 minutes of meditation at the best time for you, and do that consistently for three weeks before you lengthen your meditation. If you are finding it difficult to get started, try this writing exercise.

What is holding me back from meditating?

1. ....
....
2. ....
....
3. ....
....
4. ....
....
5. ....
....

What practical things can I do to get past these blocks?

1...
....
2...
....
3...
....
4...
....
5...
....

If a particular emotion comes up when you resist getting started—you've found your first negative emotion to meditate on!

Learning to Meditate

Getting Started

Here is a simple step-by-step technique to get you started.

- Choose somewhere to relax—either sitting or lying down. Make sure you won't be interrupted.
- Wear comfy clothes, and make sure you aren't too warm or too cold.
  - If needed, play some quiet background music—nothing with lyrics.

RELAX YOUR BODY

Settle in place and begin to relax your muscles. An easy way to do this is to contract them first. Start with your head and face—frown, screw up your face, and squeeze! Then release and feel the difference. Now move down the rest of your body, starting at the top:

- Face
- Neck and shoulders
- Arms
- Hands
- Pelvis
- Thighs
- Calves
- Feet and toes

As you do this exercise, breathe deeply and slowly, in and out through your nose.

FOCUS ON FEELING

This simple meditation helps you notice your emotions and let them go.

- How does that emotion make you feel?
- Are you feeling it somewhere in your body?
- Imagine the feeling getting smaller and drifting away until it has fully disappeared.
- Relax for as long as you are comfortable, breathing deeply.
- Let your awareness slowly come back until you feel ready to go about your day.

Here is an example: "This is sorrow—this is how it feels—I feel it in my throat and chest."

This process will help you understand how you respond to individual emotions, while noticing that they are separate from you. You may need to address the same emotion or situation many times to fully deal with it. Be patient, move slowly, and you will make progress.

REFLECT ON YOUR EMOTIONS

This meditation helps you notice tension in your body, as well as working out why certain emotions have come up.

- Sit or lie down for a moment; then breathe deeply so you begin to feel calm and relaxed.
- Breathe in through your nose for a count of five; then breathe out through your nose for a count of five. Inhale and exhale as deeply as you can.
- Tune in to your body—where are you holding tension? Breathe into it and let it go.
- Turn your attention to your emotions. Identify them one by one, and acknowledge that they are there and what they feel like. Tell yourself that you can let them go.
- Spend some time reflecting on how each emotion started and why you feel that way.
- Now that you understand the emotion, you can let go of the need to control it.
- Return to your breath, and relax for a few minutes before slowly bringing your attention back to the room.

Some people like
to add visualization to their
meditation to work through things
that have happened. For example, you
could imagine someone you really
admire and visualize how they
might deal with a situation.

From Meditation to
Mindfulness

When feelings of calm and positivity begin to seep out of your meditation routine and into your life, you are on your way to experiencing mindfulness!

Sometimes it is easier to introduce mindfulness when you don't have to concentrate. Try it when you are sitting with a cup of tea. Really appreciate the taste, the feel, and the warmth of the cup. When you are reading a book, totally immerse yourself in the story. If you are cooking a meal, appreciate the scents, textures, and how everything comes together in the finished dish.

The next time you find yourself slipping into feelings of being overwhelmed by thoughts or distracted by mobile devices, take the time to stop and focus on just one thing—even if it is as simple as how your hand feels.

An A–Z of Mindful Thinking

This A–Z includes techniques, ideas, and areas of your life that you can focus on to help you live more mindfully.

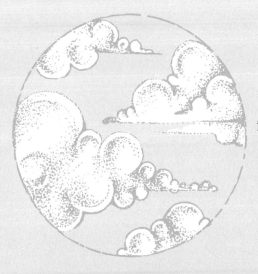

AIR

Some people love to meditate in the outdoors. They enjoy feeling the wind on their skin while focusing on the present moment. It is also great for getting fresh air!

ACKNOWLEDGMENT

You should never judge yourself for feeling an emotion. If you feel angry, you feel angry! If you can acknowledge that you feel a particular emotion and then let it go, it does not control you. Once you've repeated this with a range of emotions, you will begin to find them easier to release.

BREATHING

Slow, deep breathing is one of the most relaxing things you can do, and it is an important part of meditation. Breathe in slowly and deeply for a count of five; then breathe out fully for a count of five. If you find it hard to take deep breaths to start with, go as slowly as you can. This is something that you can do at any time of the day.

CARING

Doing something kind or caring for others can make a huge difference in how you feel. Don't forget that it is just as important to care for yourself.

DECISION-MAKING

Because mindfulness helps you to detach from raw emotions, it can help you make clearer decisions. If you need to decide something, you can examine how you feel about each of your options during a meditation.

EPHEMERAL

It is easy to believe that a difficult phase will go on forever, but it is important to understand that change is always on its way. If you can see that something will change and that a solution will be found, it can help soften anxiety. This can give you the strength to move forward.

FRAGRANCE

Some people like to use incense, flowers, or a scented candle when they are meditating. Scents such as lavender, ylang-ylang, and jasmine are relaxing and soothing.

GARDENING

Gardening is amazing for mindfulness! It's easy to become totally absorbed in digging, weeding, or dead-heading—plus you get all that fresh air.

GUILT

Guilt is a difficult emotion that often binds itself to other emotions, such as anger. Meditation is a great way to un-stitch guilt from other feelings. Acknowledge it, notice what it feels like, and then let it go. It is what you do after you feel guilty that matters the most.

HOLDING ON

Holding on to negative emotions only leads to one thing: churning over the same thoughts and scenarios again and again. Think of an emotion that you are holding on to—perhaps a sense of longing for life to be different. Go into meditation and think about your emotions. There may also be sadness, frustration, and grief. Once you have acknowledged the full range of your emotions, you can begin to look at your situation more logically.

IMAGINATION

Both observation and visualization can activate the imagination. Try visualizing a beautiful garden—plan the layout, plant the trees, smell the flowers. Make it as detailed as possible. Enjoy all the details, and return to this place in your mind as often as you like!

I AM …

Do not judge yourself for feeling a particular way. You are who you are—and that's OK. The more relaxed you can feel about being yourself, the more open you will be to other people. Dealing with difficult emotions during meditation is a great way to accept all the parts of you.

JUDGMENT

Whatever issue you are considering, if you are judging yourself or someone else, you are unlikely to find a solution. Meditate. Step back. Look at what happened without judgment. Identify your emotions and how they make you feel; then let them go.

JEALOUSY

This emotion is called the "green-eyed monster." It comes up when we suspect that someone else (normally a rival) is replacing us in some way. Through meditation you can work out why you feel jealous, if you have a reason to feel that way, and how to move forward—perhaps by explaining how you feel to someone without blaming them. Mastering this emotion can be super tough, but it is worth it.

KALEIDOSCOPE

A kaleidoscope is a good metaphor for all the moving, swirling thoughts inside a person's mind. Remember, only you oversee how the patterns change!

LIGHTING

Some people find they need a calming atmosphere to meditate. Bright sunlight, dappled shade, dim lighting, or darkness can help you get into a peaceful meditative state. What works best for you?

MUSIC

Some people like to meditate in silence, while others prefer natural sounds, such as bird songs or rainfall. Others love soft, rhythmic music without lyrics.

NATURE

Observing nature is a beautiful way to find mindfulness. Start with a leaf or twig. Give it all your attention. Look at its patterns and feel its textures. This will help you become more present in other areas of your life.

OVERTHINKING

This is the root cause of many problems! If something has made you angry or upset, do you keep going over it in your head? All this does is let the conflict take control. Meditate and watch whatever is bothering you as if you were looking at someone else. Seek forgiveness for yourself and anyone else involved. "Take away the complaint, I have been harmed, and the harm is taken away," is one of Marcus Aurelius' most famous quotes.

PEER PRESSURE

Whenever you are choosing to buy something or do anything for yourself, consider its value to you and how it represents your personality—not about what others think of it.

QUIET

When you sit down to meditate, you notice that nowhere is truly silent. You might hear the wind in the trees, the ripple of water, the cry of a bird, or the barking of a dog. Or it might be the sound of a car or a mobile device. Start noticing all the details.

QUALITY TIME

The time you spend with those closest to you is quality time. Forget distractions and your to-do list, and focus on enjoying your time with the people you love.

REST

Mindfulness can help you find a restful state. Sleep is important for our health and well-being, so try meditating before bed if you have trouble dropping off.

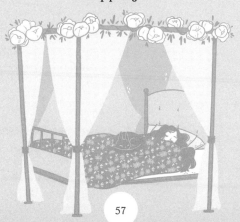

SENSORY AWARENESS

Choose an object, such as a stone, flower, or spiderweb. Concentrate on it until you feel completely absorbed in all of its details. This is a great way to get into the feeling of meditation.

TRAVEL

Everyone loves a trip! But not everyone enjoys coming back home and slipping back into their routine. If you stay mindful, you'll be able to recall experiences in your imagination when you return home—and use meditation to travel in your mind. Mindfulness helps you focus on the good in your life rather than the idea that the grass is always greener on the other side.

UNBALANCED

When looking for ways to improve your life, examine areas that are out of balance. You may be studying too much and not resting enough. Use mindfulness to ponder your options, without judgment or emotion, and find ways to reduce stress.

VICIOUS CIRCLE

If you are reliving a negative event from the past, you will likely expect every similar situation to turn out the same way. The more negative the outcome in the past, the bigger a negative impact it is going to have on the present. Mindfulness helps us to stop projecting our worries into the future.

VISUALIZATION

Visualization is great for boosting self-confidence. Start by breathing deeply and relaxing. Focus on

a situation you wish had been different. Imagine someone you admire being by your side, helping you. How would they have reacted? Keep replaying the scene, but now see yourself coping with calm confidence. Next time you encounter a similar situation, you will be better prepared to deal with it.

WALKING

Walking is a great way to get some exercise—and to start observing your environment. At some point on your walk, stop and reflect for a few moments. Focus on one thing you have found of interest, or focus on nothing and just relax. Look for beauty!

XENOPHILE

A xenophile is someone who loves foreign things and people. When you meditate, you need to open your mind to new experiences that can change and broaden your life. Introduce yourself to your inner xenophile, and get curious about the people and objects that are foreign to your personal experiences. This open-mindedness allows you to be curious about uncomfortable things that happen, rather than reacting to them immediately with anger or fear.

YOGA

Yoga is physical movement that involves the body, mind, and spirit. There are many different types of yoga that can help you on your mindfulness journey.

ZEN

Zen is a school of Buddhism that developed in China in the sixth century. One of its main teachings is to not worry about things over which you have no influence or control. The word Zen has come to mean calm and relaxed.

Spells for Mindfulness

Mindful Spells

Now that you've learned the basics of mindfulness and meditation, you can continue harnessing your natural ability to be mindful daily. This next section contains a series of spells that help you do just that!

Spells, incantations, and charms are all wonderful ways to improve your well-being and bring positive change into your life!

Once you've mastered the ability to be mindful, you are ready for successful spell-making. This is because mindfulness brings a heightened sense of awareness about what you are experiencing, as well as putting your attention on what you are thinking, feeling, and doing at the time—and what you'd like to manifest next!

WHAT ARE SPELLS?

In ancient communities, the elders—or wise ones—had access to certain knowledge (and power) that was not available to most people. This is because they had so much life experience. They also knew that the way we speak matters.

There are three important things to remember when using spells:

- Words spoken with intensity and passion have a power of their own.
- The speaker has a power and energy that they can learn to use effectively.
- There are forces and powers beyond our understanding that can be used or directed for specific purposes.

Types of Spells

There are several kinds of spell, and they all require a different approach.

LOVE SPELLS

Love spells are ways to make someone find another person attractive. Love spells should be unconditional and free from self-interest.

BIDDING SPELLS

These spells command a particular thing to happen, but without the cooperation of others; therefore, spells must only be cast for the highest good of all.

BLESSINGS

These can be prayers or spells. They require concentration to bring peace or healing to the recipient. They are considered positive energy from beyond the spell-maker, being directed toward a specific purpose.

HEALING SPELLS AND CHARMS

These spells ask for general healing of all levels.

INVOCATIONS

These call on what is believed to be the ultimate source of power, which differs from spell to spell. An invocation calls up that power and asks for permission to use its influence for a specific reason.

Spells for selfish power, or to gain power over others, will often backfire and cause damage to whomever casts them; however, invocations of positive forces do no harm.

THE INCANTATION

This type of spell appeals to gods, goddesses, and the powers of nature for help.

Getting Ready

There are several ways to prepare for spell work, from bathing and choosing what to wear to setting up your altar.

An altar is a surface (such as a small table) that holds objects such as candles, flowers, and crystals. They are used to increase a particular energy and should be in a quiet place where candles can be burned safely.

RITUAL BATHS

Some spells require you to take a ritual bath to cleanse your energy so you can get the best results from your magic work (see pages 70–71). As you mix your salts into your bath, bless the water and charge it with your intention. During a ritual bath, you will place candles safely around you. The shade of the candles you choose relates to your intention.

Use pink candles for calm, blue candles for wisdom, and green candles for self-awareness.

Red candles work for energy, and purple candles are for spiritual matters.

MINDFUL SPELL-CASTING

Be aware of the sights, sounds, smells, and tastes of the present moment as you go through the steps of each spell. Doing this will help you experience things in a mindful way.

For the spells in this book, there is a list of ingredients and items that may be required to achieve a particular result. Because every spell-maker brings their own energy to the process, you may find that you want to change something. That is fine! Make the spells your own!

YOU WILL NEED:

- A handful of homemade bath salts (made from three parts Epsom salts, two parts baking soda, one part rock salt—all mixed together)
- Candles in the shade that best suits your intention
- A large white candle and a lighter
- Rosemary essential oil (to remove negativity)
- A large glass of mineral water

METHOD:

- First, anoint the white candle with the essential oil by rubbing a few drops onto its surface. Ask for positivity, health, and happiness as you do so. Do the same to your other candles.
- Run your bath, and mix in the bath salts.
- Light the white candle first; then light the others.
- Place the candles safely around the bath.
- Lie back and enjoy your bath.
- Drink the mineral water, and imagine that your whole body is being cleansed inside and out.
- Thank the water for preparing you for new energies.
- If you are about to perform a magical working, keep your mind focused on your intention.
- When you've finished your bath, carefully put out the candles.

Health and Healing

A Spell for Good Health

This spell works best if performed during the New Moon. Bay leaves possess magical power and are used for granting wishes. In this spell, they are used to bring health and happiness! Remember: spells are not a substitute for professional medical care.

YOU WILL NEED:

- 3 bay leaves
- A sheet of paper
- A pencil or pen

METHOD:

- Write your wish on the paper; imagine it coming true.
- Fold the paper into thirds, placing three bay leaves inside.
- Fold the paper toward you, still imagining your wish.
- Fold the paper into thirds a second time.
- Hide it in a dark place, and continue your visualizations.
- When your wish comes true, destroy the paper as a means to give thanks.

"Healing may not be so much about getting better, as about letting go of everything that isn't you—all of the expectations, all of the beliefs—and becoming who you are."
—Rachel Naomi Remen

Sleep Well

Often called the dream stone, smoky quartz, is used to help release emotions like grief, anger, and despair.

YOU WILL NEED:

- A piece of smoky quartz
- A piece of paper and a pen
- Your bed

METHOD:

- Before bed, sit quietly holding the smoky quartz.
- Let any feelings of hurt, anger, or difficulty come up (so they can be let go).
- Put the quartz to one side, and write down everything you thought about and felt.
- Imagine a large infinity symbol (∞) over your bed.
- Pass the quartz over the bed three times, following this shape.
- Wrap the quartz in the paper; place it under your pillow, with an intention that it will help with your pain or hurt.
- Go to sleep. In the morning, remove the paper and destroy it. Repeat for two more nights.
- Cleanse the crystal under running water. Keep it safe until you need it again.

Healing the Body

This spell helps you discover whether a pain you are experiencing is physical, emotional, or spiritual. It calls on Raphael the Archangel of healing for help.

YOU WILL NEED:

- A large piece of paper
- Red, yellow, and purple felt-tip pens
- A black marker

METHOD:

- Draw three concentric circles—the inner circle should be purple, the middle should be yellow, and the outer should be red.
- Add another circle at the top to represent your head, and two lines below for your legs.
- Think of any health difficulties you have. Hold the paper with the circles in one hand and the black marker in the other. While reciting the spell, make a small mark somewhere on the circles to represent your pain. Ask Raphael for help:

RAPHAEL, RAPHAEL, ANGEL OF EASE, HELP ME UNDERSTAND THIS PAIN, PLEASE.

- You should find that your mark is closest to one of the circles. The red circle represents pain that is physical; the yellow circle signifies emotional pain; purple represents spiritual pain.
- Sit quietly, and imagine that hue covering the area where you are experiencing pain.
- Next, imagine that part of your body flooding with white light.
- Repeat the invocation to Raphael twice more over the next two days—and repeat the drawing in of your chosen hue and flooding of white light.
- Journal any insights about the causes of your pain.

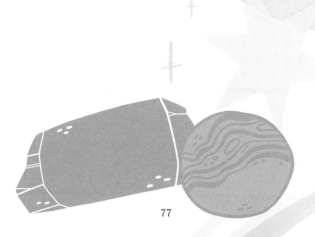

Releasing Negative Emotion

This technique helps with negative energies, such as anger or resentment, and clears the way for manifesting.

YOU WILL NEED:

- A dark stone

METHOD:

- Visualize a circle of light around you while holding the stone. Place the stone over your solar plexus (upper belly, in front of the diaphragm).
- Allow the negative energy to flow into the stone.
- Ask yourself how the emotion arose and what hue it is.
- Imagine the appearance of the stone changing.
- Raise the stone to your forehead to signify clarity.
- Next, place it over your heart.
- To reinforce the idea that the stone holds your emotions, speak these words:

WITH THIS STONE,
NEGATIVE BE GONE.
LET WATER CLEANSE IT,
BACK WHERE IT BELONGS.

- Concentrate on projecting your negative emotion into the stone.
- Take the stone to a source of running water in the open air, such as a river or ocean. With all your energy, throw it into the water.

Purify Emotions

This modified spell will help you let go of old situations. It should be performed during the Waning Moon phase.

YOU WILL NEED:

- A white candle (lit)
- A bowl of water
- A bowl of salt

METHOD:

- Stand in front of your altar and say, "I call upon the elements in this simple ceremony that I may be cleansed of the contamination of negativity."
- Wave your hands over the lit candle (stay well above the flame so you don't get burned). Say these words: "I willingly release negative action in my fire."
- Rub salt on your hands and say, "I release stumbling blocks and obstacles in my earth."
- Think about any upcoming moments that you'll need clarity. Dip your hands in the water and say, "I purify this water; let this relinquishing be gentle. Purified, cleansed, and released in all ways. I now acknowledge my trust and faith in my own clarity."
- Dispose of the ingredient outdoors in the earth. Pour the water on the ground so it mingles with the salt.

Enhance Confidence

This spell uses noise to spark confidence!

YOU WILL NEED:

- A bell or rattle
- Music that excites you—perhaps with drumming
  - Your voice!

METHOD:

Choose an affirmation that describes how you want to feel, such as "I can overcome any problem" or "I have the confidence to do anything!"

- Choose a time and place when you won't disturb others—and you won't be disturbed.
- Play your music until you feel uplifted.
- Pick up your bell or rattle, and dance!
- Recite your affirmation loudly at least three times—preferably nine.
- Think of three things that you can do over the next week that can demonstrate your newfound confidence. Imagine doing them with the energy you now have in your body.
- Repeat every week!

Helping Others

This spell uses crystals, candles, and incense. The paper represents the person you are helping to heal.

YOU WILL NEED:

- Three candles: blue for healing, white for power, and pink for love
- Healing incense, such as sandalwood
- A piece of paper with the name of the person you wish to be healed
- A clear quartz crystal
- A lighter

METHOD:

- Place the candles on your altar in a semi-circle, with the white candle in the middle.
- If the person you wish to help is female, place the incense on the left of the altar; if they are male, place it on the right.
- Light the incense.
- Place the piece of paper in the middle, and put the quartz on top of the paper.
- Breathe deeply, close your eyes, and become aware of whatever you consider to be the Divine.

- Smell the incense and feel your energy increasing.
- When you are ready, imagine this energy passing from you, through the crystal, to the recipient. As you are doing this, say:

[PERSON'S NAME],
BE HEALED BY THE GIFT
OF THIS POWER.

A physical condition may not necessarily be healed by this spell, but you may well help start the process. Sometimes, the person is given the emotional strength to cope with their health issues, so that an inner healing begins.

Love Spells

Attract Love

When you use this spell, you are imagining what it is like to be in love—and you set up a current of energy to attract it.

YOU WILL NEED:

- A sprig of rosemary
- A rose quartz crystal
- Rose incense
- Pink candle
- Small box
- A red pen

> "The most precious gift we can offer others is our presence. When mindfulness embraces those we love, they will bloom like flowers."
> —Thich Nhat Hanh

METHOD:

- Sit somewhere that feels powerful to you, such as in front of your altar, near a tree, or next to running water.
- Write "Love is mine" on the box.
- Light your incense, and place the rosemary and quartz in the box.
- Let the incense burn out.
- Seal the box shut to contain the vibration of love. Don't open it until you have found your true love.
- When love has found you, take the quartz out from the box, and keep it as a reminder.
- Bury the box in the earth.

Clearing the Air

Use this spell when communication between you and someone you love feels difficult.

YOU WILL NEED:

- A crystal ball or a magnifying glass
- A photograph of the other person

METHOD:

- Place the crystal ball or magnifying glass over the photo—see their features get bigger and appear to move.
- State your wishes or difficulties—and what the other person can do to help you.

For your person to get the message, you'll need to trust that you can be a transmitter and know that you are trying to help them understand how you feel—not change them.

Friendship

This spell helps you call in new friends. It works best during the New Moon.

YOU WILL NEED:

- Several sheets of paper and a pen
- A few drops of jasmine, lavender, or patchouli essential oil mixed into almond oil
- A white candle and a lighter

METHOD:

- Rub a few drops of the oil onto the candle.
- Draw a symbol on the candle that represents friendship to you; then light it.
- Take a ritual bath (see page 68).
- After the bath, place a few drops of the oil on the inside of your wrists.
- On a sheet of paper, draw a figure to represent yourself; then describe yourself, including the qualities that make you a good friend.
- On the other pieces of paper, draw figures to represent the types of people you would like to meet.
- Hold your piece of paper against each of the "friend" papers, so that they "meet" face to face.
  Each time, say these words:

LET US MEET EACH OTHER,
LET US GREET EACH OTHER.
LET US BECOME FRIENDS,
LET US BECOME COMPANIONS.
AND IF WE GROW TO LOVE ONE
ANOTHER, THEN SO BE IT.

- Put a drop of the oil on one corner of each paper.
- Spread the papers out in front of you, and visualize a link from you to each of the others, like a spiderweb. Say:

SPIDER WOMAN, SPIDER WOMAN,
WEAVE ME A CHARM;
MAKE ME GOOD ENOUGH,
SMART ENOUGH,
THEM ALL TO DISARM.

- Let the candle burn out.
- New friends should appear before the next New Moon!

Life can be seen as a network—and everyone is a strand within that network. Spider Woman is a North American goddess who weaves charm and reveals the power and purpose of each strand.

To Let Go of Someone

Not all relationships last, and sometimes we can be left with bad feelings about another person. This spell helps you release those feelings.

YOU WILL NEED:

- A photo of the person
- A bulb of garlic
- A red bag or cloth

METHOD:

- Place the picture of the person you wish to release in front of you.
- Gather up all your hurt and pain, and tear the picture into small pieces.
- Feel the emotions flowing away from you as you say the words:

LEAVE MY HEART, LEAVE ME FREE;
LEAVE MY LIFE, NO PAIN FOR ME.
AS THIS PICTURE IS TORN TO DUST,
HELP ME NOW, MOVE ON I MUST.

- Repeat these words until the picture is torn up completely.
- Take the garlic, and hold it to your solar plexus (the top of your stomach)
- Allow any bad feelings to flow into the garlic bulb.
- Touch the root to your forehead to indicate that you have converted the bad feelings to good.
- Send the person loving thoughts.
- Wrap everything in the red bag or cloth—then bury it as far from your home as you can.

Find New Love

Perform this spell during a New Moon. Everything you use should be brand new.

YOU WILL NEED:

- A clean sheet of red paper or card
- A clean sheet of white paper
- A new pen
- A new pink candle and a new lighter
- A new envelope

METHOD:

- On the day of a New Moon, cut a heart from the red paper or card.
- On the white paper, write: "As this heart shines in candlelight, I draw you to me tonight."
- Take a ritual bath (see page 68), and change into your PJs.
- Light the candle and read the invocation out loud.
- Hold the heart in front of the flame, and let the candlelight shine onto it.
- Place the heart and spell in the envelope—seal it with wax from the candle.
- Put the envelope in a safe place; leave it untouched for one Moon cycle.
- When the Moon is new again, there should be a new love in your life.

To Beckon a Person

This is a simple way to put out a vibration, which, if a relationship has a chance of succeeding, can make the other person aware of you. Remember, a loving friend is just as important as a romantic love interest.

METHOD:
Say the following:

I MOVE TO YOU,
AS YOU MOVE TO ME.
AS I THINK OF YOU,
THINK ALSO OF ME.
AS I CALL YOUR NAME,
CALL ME TO YOU.
COME TO ME IN LOVE.

Say the person's name three times. You may need to say the spell a few times to feel its full effect.

Wealth and Luck

Attracting Extra Money

It may seem like mindfulness and money have nothing to do with each other, but our state of mind does affect our wealth, as well as our ability to attract luck into our lives.

Use this spell outside at night during the New Moon.

YOU WILL NEED:

- Loose change

METHOD:

- Gaze up at the Moon.
- Turn your money over in your pocket.
- As you do so, repeat the following three times:

"Your vision will become clear only when you look into your heart. Who looks outside, dreams; who looks inside, awakens."
—Carl Jung

GODDESS OF LIGHT AND LOVE, I PRAY,
BRING FORTUNE UNTO ME THIS DAY.

You will know the spell has worked when you come across money unexpectedly!

More Money Spell

This spell, performed around the Full Moon, helps improve your attitude toward money. There are two versions—one that burns money and one that does not. This version does not burn money.

YOU WILL NEED:

- A green taper candle with candleholder
- A pin
- Mint or honeysuckle oil
- A bank note (either real or play money)

METHOD:

- Two days before the Full Moon, place the candle in the holder on the altar. Carve currency symbols on it using the pin, while imagining a prosperous life.
- Rub the essential oil into the candle; then light.
- Place the money in front of the candle. Think about your feelings about money and how you'd spend it.
- The next night, light the candle again, and visualize your money increasing.
- On the third night, place the money somewhere safe or—if it's real—donate it. But do not spend it on yourself!

Want Spell

This spell reminds you that Mother Nature supplies you with all your basic needs.

YOU WILL NEED:

- A marker
- A fully grown leaf that has fallen from a tree

METHOD:

- On the leaf, draw a word, picture, or letter that represents the thing that you want.
- Lay the leaf on the ground.
- As the leaf withers, it takes your desire to the Earth. In thanks, Mother Nature will grant your wish.
- If you don't want to leave it on the ground, you may also throw it into running water, or place it under a stone.

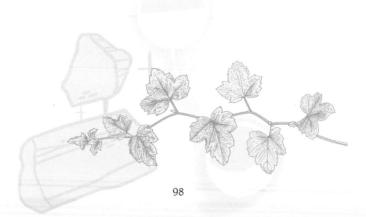

Candles and Pennies

Fire and finance go together—so a candle spell using pennies is a good way of drawing money toward you. Green shades are traditionally used in money spells.

YOU WILL NEED:

- A green candle and a lighter
- Glass tumbler
- Enough small coins to fill half of the glass
- A pin

METHOD:

- Fill the glass with the coins to the halfway point.
- Draw the rune symbol for Fehu on the candle using a pin. Fehu stands for fortune and completion.
- Put the candle in the glass.
- Light the candle, and let it burn down so that the wax mixes with the pennies. As you light the candle, say that you only want what is needed, nothing more.
- Place the glass in a safe space and allow the candle to burn out.

The idea behind this spell is that the money will stick to you!

Banish Your Debts

This spell uses candle and incense magic! It is best performed at the time of the Waning Moon.

YOU WILL NEED:

- A small piece of paper no wider than 5 cm (2 in)
- A black pen
- A pin
- A purple candle and a lighter
- A large, heatproof candleholder
- An essential oil of your choice
- An incense of your choice

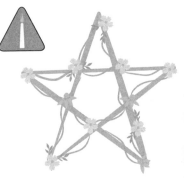

METHOD:

- Light the incense, and rub a dab of oil on the side of the candle.
- List all your debts on the paper, and then fold it up.
- Draw a banishing pentagram on the back of the paper (see illustration above).
- Draw another banishing pentagram on the candle using the pin.
- Place the folded paper on the altar; then place the candleholder on top of the paper.
- Concentrate on banishing your debts, and visualize your happiness and relief when this happens.

- Light the candle, and then face East. Ask the Spirit of Air to acknowledge your intention to be debt-free.
- In your own words, ask for your debts to be banished and replaced with prosperity.
- Allow the candle to burn out completely.
- Feel the feeling of debt being lifted from the paper and into the candle as the candle burns down.
- Destroy the paper after you've finished.

You shouldn't expect your debts to simply disappear, but the ability to clear them should come quickly in the form of a gift or an opportunity for some extra work. Once your debts are cleared, make sure you don't create the same problem again.

Success and Decision-Making

Finding a Job

When thinking about your future, mindfulness can help you make the best of what you have in order to maximize your potential.

> "Now is the future you promised yourself last year, last month, last week. Now is the only moment you'll ever really have. Mindfulness is about waking up to this."
> —Mark Williams

If you are thinking about getting your first job, try this spell. The incense mixture (below) must be made beforehand.

Incense Recipe

- 1 teaspoon ground cinnamon
- 1 teaspoon ground ginger
- 1 teaspoon ground lemon balm
- A few drops of bergamot oil

Mix all the ingredients in your bowl

YOU WILL NEED:

- Your job application form (not yet filled in)
- A tiger's eye crystal
- Talcum power
- Bowl
- Incense mixture (see opposite page)
- Charcoal disc
- Heatproof incense burner

METHOD:

- Burn the incense on top of a charcoal disc in the heatproof burner. Ask an adult to help you.
- Before you fill in the application, hold the paper in the incense smoke. Ask for a blessing for the process you are about to start.
- Place the tiger's eye crystal on your desk.
- Fill in the application.
- Sprinkle the talcum powder on the back of each page of the form.
- Draw your four fingers though the powder in wavy lines from top to bottom so they leave clear tracks.
- Leave for a few moments; then shake off the powder. While you do this, visualize your success.
- Place the form on your altar overnight.

Open Sesame

Sesame seeds are said to have the power to open locks, reveal hidden passages, and find hidden treasures. Here they are used to attract good pay!

YOU WILL NEED:

- A ceramic or glass bowl
- A handful of sesame seeds

METHOD:

- Place the sesame seeds in the bowl.
- Put the bowl near the door of your home in a safe space.

- Each time you pass the bowl on your way out, give it a stir with your right ring finger.
- Change the seeds every month. Throw the old ones away by burying them or dropping them into running water.

You can also place sesame seed oil on the inside of your wrists for extra support at a job interview!

Find Your Talents

This charm will help you develop your potential.
Perform it during a Crescent Moon.

YOU WILL NEED:

- A small drawstring bag, about 2.5–5 cm
  (1–2 in) deep, and a ball of string
- Licorice root powder
- Rose hips
- Fennel
- Elderflower

METHOD:

- Put a pinch or two of the herbs in the bag
- Hang the bag outside at sunset.
- At midnight, remove the bag. Tie it to some string
  and wear it loosely around your neck.
- Say this affirmation before you sleep:

AS I SLEEP, I SHALL LEARN OF MY BEST POTENTIAL.

- Wear the charm bag for 24 hours and place it under
  your pillow any time you need some extra help
  reaching your goals.

Decision-Making

Do this spell at the New Moon if a new beginning is involved.

YOU WILL NEED:

- Two yellow candles
- A white candle
- A length of purple ribbon, about 60 cm (2 ft) long
- Two pieces of paper
- A pen
- A lighter

METHOD:

- Lay out the ribbon on a flat surface, and place the white candle exactly in the middle. Place the two yellow candles on either end.
- Write the two possible outcomes on the pieces of paper, and fold them separately. Place them under the yellow candles.
- Light the white candle first; then light the two yellow ones. Acknowledge that you will be extinguishing them as part of the spell.
- Let the candles burn for at least one hour (stay with them while they are burning). During that time, consider both options carefully.
- Extinguish the candles.

- The next day, move the papers and yellow candles closer to the middle candle. Roll the ribbon in toward them.
- Light the candles and burn them again for at least one hour.
- Repeat every day until all the candles are together (this should take at least three days).
- Allow the candles to completely burn out. You should now find it easy to decide!

Concentration

This spell calls on the powers of Bridget, the goddess of poetry.

YOU WILL NEED:

- A small cloth bag and silver thread
- Herb mixture: two-parts rosemary, two-parts basil, one-part caraway seeds, one-part dried citrus rind (lemon or lime)

METHOD:

- Combine the herbs thoroughly while chanting these words:

BRIDGET, BRIGHDE FASHIONER
OF WORDS, HELP ME NOW AS I SEEK YOUR
AID, LET ME NOW BRING
YOU THANKS IN WHAT
I HAVE TO SAY TODAY.

- Put the herbs in the bag and tie it with the silver thread.
- Place it on your desk where you can see it.

Focusing on the bag helps free your mind as you study. If you feel stuck, open the bag and allow some of the fragrance to escape—just remember to tie it up again!

Remove Misfortune

This spell uses plant magic to remove misfortune.
When you become aware of any misfortune you are
facing, look for a common theme and name it as part
of the spell.

YOU WILL NEED:

- 3 small glass jars
- 9 cloves of garlic
- 9 pins

METHOD:

- Pierce the cloves of garlic with the pins, while
  saying the following with confidence:

MISFORTUNE, BEGONE FROM ME

- Put three of the garlic cloves and pins in each jar.
- Bury each jar somewhere meaningful, such as next to a
  river or under a tree.
- Walk away and—most importantly—don't look
  back. Leave your misfortune behind!

Long-term Security

This spell takes about one week to perform. Before you begin, consider your attitude toward money and focus on truly believing that you are abundant. This spell is designed for long-term security.

YOU WILL NEED:

- 7 silver coins
- a small bowl
- a green candle
- a candleholder

METHOD:

- Place the candle, candleholder, and bowl on a flat surface in an area that you will walk past every day.
- Every day for seven days, place a coin in the bowl.
- After seven days, take the candle and spend time imagining prosperity coming to you. What does it feel like? Sense the new opportunities that await you!
- Place the candle in the holder.
- Place the seven coins in your left hand and close your fingers. While holding the coins, move your hand in a circle.
- Put one coin in front of the candle.
  As you place it down, say:

MONEY GROW, MAKE IT MINE; MONEY FLOW, MONEY'S MINE.

- Place the other coins around the candle, and repeat the incantation for each one.
- Light the candle and allow it to burn out.
- Leave the money in position for at least three days, and do not spend it!

A Potpourri
of Spells!

To Travel Safely

This spell is to help protect your luggage and yourself before a journey.

YOU WILL NEED:

- A sprig of rosemary
- A purple ribbon
- Four tea light candles
- A few drops of sandalwood oil

METHOD:

- Place the rosemary on top of your luggage.
- Trace a pentagram over each lock. Weave the ribbon securely around the handle.
- Say the following three times:

PROTECTED IS THIS CASE OF MINE, RETURN NOW SAFELY IN GOOD TIME.

- The night before you travel, take a bath, placing tea lights at each corner of the tub. Add the essential oil to the water. Visualize all your cares being washed away. Concentrate on the journey to come, without any worry.

- Blow out the tea lights when you have finished your bath.

A Ring of Protection

In this spell, you place a protective shield of light around your home. All you need is the power of your mind.

METHOD:

- Visualize a ring of light surrounding your house.
- Ask for your guardian angels to protect your home and everyone who lives there.
- Reinforce the circle of light whenever you think about it—it's that simple!

"Change the future by changing the present. Don't wait to start. Start now."
—Akiroq Brost

Reverse Negativity

Using mindful spells to protect our personal space creates a feeling of calm, while banishing negative energies. This spell can be used to deal with anger that is being directed at you.

YOU WILL NEED:

- A purple candle
- Rosemary oil
- White paper
- A pen with black ink
- A fireproof dish

> "Feelings, whether of compassion or irritation, should be welcomed, recognized, and treated on an absolutely equal basis, because both are ourselves."
> —Thich Nhat Hanh

METHOD:

- Visualize the blocks in your life being removed, while rubbing a dab of oil into your candle.
- On the paper, write the following: My blocks are removed.
- Fold the paper three times away from you. Light the candle, and burn the paper in the dish (ask for an adult's help with this). Repeat the following three times:

FIREDRAKES AND SALAMANDERS,
AID ME IN MY QUEST,
PROTECT ME FROM ALL EVIL THOUGHTS.

- After the final repetition, say: "Let it be so."

Find Something Lost

This spell will help you find something you have lost, particularly if it is nearby. Normally, a pendulum is used to answer questions with a yes or a no. Here you take note of the direction it swings.

YOU WILL NEED:

- A pendulum—this could be a crystal on a short chain, a ring tied to a thread, or similar

METHOD:

- Visualize the object you have lost, and focus on why you need it.
- Hold the pendulum in your writing hand, and support your elbow on a flat surface.
- Allow the pendulum to move, sensing which direction it pulls toward the most.
- Try a few times to see if it pulls the same way. If so, your item could be in that direction. Repeat until you get closer to your object.

Sometimes, an object will be lost for good—it will reappear in its own time, if you really need it.

Knot Spells

This spell uses knots to hold energy—either to prevent something from happening or to make something happen at a certain time.

YOU WILL NEED:

- A short length of string, ribbon, or fabric strip

METHOD:

- Before you start, reflect on why you want to influence a particular situation. Remember, that you should never try to force someone to do something against their will.
- Tie a simple knot using your string or ribbon. As you do, say these words:

AS THIS KNOT IS TIED IN THEE,
THE POWER IS HELD UNTIL SET FREE.
'TIS BOUND, UNTIL ON MY COMMAND,
THE KNOWLEDGE NEEDED COMES
AS PLANNED.

- Put the tied object in your pocket and on the morning of an important event, undo the knot at your chosen moment. This will allow you to have all the information and energy you need for success!

- You can use this same spell to enhance your dreams. For example, if you wish to find the answer to a problem as you sleep, hold the material in your hand and allow your energy to flow into it.
- Tie a simple knot while saying:

CATCH NOW MY DREAMS,
AND HOLD THEM STILL.
THAT I MAY KNOW WHAT IS THY WILL.
CREATE A SPACE THAT I MAY SEE
WHAT ANSWER WILL BE BEST FOR ME.

- Sleep with the tied knot under your pillow, and wait for inspiration. It could take a few nights. Sometimes the answer will come outside a dream in the form of a flash of inspiration or from information from an outside source.

Slow Down

You can use this spell when things are happening too fast, or when you feel that life is running away from you.

YOU WILL NEED:

- Paper
- A pen with black ink
- A freezer

METHOD:

- On the front of the paper, either write down a few words or draw a picture of the situation you feel is moving too fast.
- On the back of the paper, draw the symbol for the planet Saturn:

♄

- Place the paper in your freezer, and leave it there until you feel you can handle your problem again.
- When you are ready, tear the paper into small pieces.

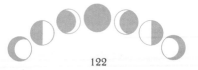

Give Encouragement

This spell allows you to work with someone without them necessarily knowing what you are doing. It is used only for positive encouragement.

YOU WILL NEED:

- A jade, rose quartz, or amethyst crystal
- Frankincense oil
- Oil burner

METHOD:

- Put the frankincense oil into the top of the burner and light it.
- Pour a couple of droplets of oil onto your hands, and rub them together to raise the power.
- Hold the crystal in your writing hand, and pass it through the fumes from the oil burner three times.
- Face the direction where you know the recipient of the spell will be and say:

GODDESS OF LOVE,
GODDESS OF POWER, HEAR ME NOW
AS I THEE IMPLORE: HELP [NAME] TO
DO WHAT THEY MUST TO CREATE THE
CONDITIONS FOR THEIR SUCCESS.

- Build up a mental ball of energy around the crystal until it is as powerful as you can make it.
- Place the crystal by the side of your bed, directing the energy of the ball toward the recipient. This energy will be sent to them in the form of self-confidence.
- Visualize the person standing tall and confident in a ray of light stretching from the crystal to them.
- The next morning, wash the crystal under running water and keep it safe.

This spell works because you have no expectations of reward. The payoff comes when you see the recipient succeed in their own way!

Index

Ask for what you want, and be prepared to get it.

MAYA ANGELOU

Other titles in the series:
Spells * Crystals * Astrology * Palm Reading *
Divination * Spells and Charms * Tarot